I0231835

The Aardvark Venus

New and Selected Poems
1961 - 2020

Rochelle Owens

texture press
2020

Also by Rochelle Owens

Poetry

Not Be Essence That Cannot Be
Four Young Lady Poets
Salt and Core
I Am the Babe of Joseph Stalin's Daughter
The Joe Eighty-Two Creation Poems
The Joe Chronicles Part 2
Shemuel
Constructs
W.C. Fields In French Light
How Much Paint Does The Painting Need
Black Chalk
Rubbed Stones and Other Poems
New and Selected Poems 1961-1996
Luca: Discourse On Life And Death
Triptych
Solitary Workwoman
Out of Ur - New & Selected Poems 1961 – 2012
Hermaphropoetics, Drifting Geometries

Plays

Futz and What Came After
The Karl Marx Play and Others
The Widow And The Colonel
Who Do You Want, Peire Vidal?
Plays by Rochelle Owens: Chucky's Hunch, Futz, Kontraption, Three Front

Fiction

Journey to Purity

Editor

Spontaneous Combustion: Eight New American Plays

Translation (French)

The Passersby, by Liliane Atlan

Film

Futz

Video

Oklahoma Too, 1987
How Much Paint Does the Painting Need, 1991
Black Chalk, 1994

The Aardvark Venus

New & Selected Poems

1961-2020

ISBN (e-book): 978-1-945784-10-1
ISBN (print): 978-1-945784-11-8

Texture Press
1108 Westbrooke Terrace
Norman, OK 73072

Acknowledgements

Some of these poems have appeared in the following publications:
Black Sparrow Press, Golden Handcuffs Review, Jacket2, Junction Press, Kulchur Foundation, Poems and Poetics, Texture Press and Trobar Books.

The author wishes to express her gratitude to Tony Frazer, Susan Smith Nash, Paul Naylor, James Penha, Marjorie Perloff, Jerome Rothenberg, Lou Rowan and Mark Weiss for their unwavering support.

Photograph of George Economou and Rochelle Owens by anon.

Cover and Book Design: Susan Smith Nash.

Dedication

In memory of George Economou
September 24, 1934 - May 3, 2019
and
for Margaret Harrington

Table of Contents

INTRODUCTION

As I reflect on the work of Rochelle Owens, I am sitting in isolation. Fear has crept in, as has the toxic miasmic twins of hypomanic activity of endless web conferences and loneliness. I think of Boccaccio's preface to *The Decameron*, as the author discusses individuals' personal responses to an outbreak of plague. In the Renaissance, ostensibly one could escape the plague by leaving the city and going to the countryside and waiting it out. However, eventually the plague would find one as it traversed the Silk Road in the bodies of the troubadours, pilgrims, knights, and merchants, who linked commerce, art, poetics and death.

If Boccaccio wrote to bring people together and show how individual stories and narratives paint a coherent and cohesive portrait of the whole person, Owens takes the opposite approach. She fragments the individual, finds the cubes of horror, blood, spit, and magic that form the unifying building blocks of human behavior and identity. She has never been afraid to plunge into the heart of the taboo and its attendant atrocities, from the idea of a man sexually obsessed with his pig, which becomes a powerful commentary on a dominant male's treatment of his wife (his chattel) to genocide by means of smallpox-infected blankets to weaken and conquer indigenous peoples. Owens captures these sharp-edged shards, which function as jagged pieces of broken mirrors. She inserts them into her poetry and in her plays so that they become the only authentic representations of self and society in a work. The mirroring shards challenge the genre because they point to the fact that generic expectations and embedded archetypes subvert any attempt to transcend a collectively agreed upon narrative, which is a socially mediated construct. Without the kind of approach that Owens uses, we are trapped in someone else's world, someone else's narrative. Pop culture, kitsch, parody and other supposed subversions only make that ontological cage smaller and tighter. Owens's mirroring fragments spring the trap. They let us out of the narrative and generic cages that have bound us.

I remember the first time I met Rochelle Owens. I can't believe it was so long ago! I was an enthusiastic graduate student who had been lucky enough to be awarded a spot in a week-long workshop on Russian and Italian avant-garde poetry of the early 20th century. The workshop was developed and given by renowned literary scholar, Marjorie Perloff. Perloff, who was a great admirer of Owens, spoke highly of her work, and I was soon to learn why.

It was a windy Oklahoma week in the spring of 1986, and the gusts of cool, dry wind made acrid by prairie-fires and cedar dust, were nothing in comparison with the forces of art and nature that were for me, absolutely new, absolutely intellectually liberating.

I was in my 20s, a petroleum geologist refugee from the oil industry, the mom of toddler who loved long walks in the stroller and building elaborate constructions, from castles to car washes, with blocks. While having more time with my son was very important to me, I was still struggling, thanks to the devastating economic blow that the collapse in commodities prices had dealt the industry. Everything I had known and believed in had been challenged. It was my first experience with economic apocalypse, made all the more disconcerting by the fact that the rest of the nation experienced a boom of unprecedented proportions thanks to low energy prices and across the board deregulation and privatization of state-regulated utilities.

When I met her, Owens was a recent arrival from New York City, and she spoke often about how Oklahoma surprised her with its history of support for the arts, which included Tulsa's elegant Art Deco architecture, the Tulsa Ballet, the Tulsa Opera. The elegance surface belied the darker subsurface, the oil that provided the wealth, much of which was legally owned by Native American tribes, victims of massacres, forced removals, and murder. Always a passionate, iconoclastic writer, Owens harnessed the dark Oklahoma energies she detected and then dissected.

We had completed the workshop, and there was a reading and a reception at the home of University of Oklahoma professor, Eugene Enrico, who had founded a unique chamber orchestra, the Collegium Musicum, which focused on medieval and Renaissance music, played on replicas of the original instruments.

Perloff gave a brief talk from the book, *The Futurist Moment: Avant-Garde, Avant-Guerre, and the Language of Rupture,* which we had studied in the workshop. It was thrilling, and I could completely identify with the energies of that time – wanting to completely reconfigure meaning and consciousness.

Then Owens read from *W. C. Fields in French Light* and drafts of her new work, *How Much Painting Does the Painting Need.* The fragmentary, incantatory rhythms immediately captured my attention and I was intrigued by the savagery and directness of the work. I thought of Antonin Artaud's *Theatre of Cruelty.* Owens's work explores the hyper-realism that results in the encapsulation of a gesture, an attitude, a transgression, and then it repeats it, embedding it in different configurations of the text. Further, the incantatory nature of her text functions as a powerful device that breaks apart the text into alternative realities. They are fragments that combine, recombine, and then break apart again.

After Owens's reading, I did everything I could to learn more about her work, not only poetry, but also her award-winning plays. In them, I found the creative, inspiring, fearless, risk-taking voice that had intrigued me from the beginning. Her first poems were published in the same milieu as the Beats, and I think that she was often viewed as an Expressionist Beat. Clearly, there was much of the performative as well, which one sees in *Not Be Essence that Cannot Be.*

I'm very happy that the full text of *Not Be Essence that Cannot Be* is incorporated in its entirety in this collection. First published in 1961, the poems experiment with fragmented language, syntax, and spellings. The line breaks further fragment the sentences and the ideas that flow forth. As in her later work, bodies appear, as do personae, but they are likewise chopped, segmented, and rendered grotesque and powerful. In "Dripping Thing Four Legs," the subject of the poem, a woman, has flesh and blood, but also shape-shifts into cedar, knotgrass, and serpents. The language creates a mental image of writhing, twisting, chunks of being that come in and out of focus and form. It is a poem of becoming, and also of un-becoming and unraveling, readying itself for its protean journey. When these poems were published, existentialist nihilism was the rage, as was constructivism. For the nihilists who may have suggested that essence is a social construct, Owens countered it with life – not only human life, but that of anything and everything endangered.

Her texts undergo a metamorphosis and as they do so, they construct realities. The reader is involved in this process because each constructed reality connects to the individual in a unique and different way, resulting in shifting emotions and feelings. With the feel of having shimmering surfaces, the words trigger ontological uncertainty – constantly transmuting beingness is not so much problematized as exposed. Far from the post-structuralist view that there is no such thing as pure essence and that everything is a socially mediated construct, Owens completely shatters the paradigm and creates a world where essence does indeed exist, and it can be found (and introduced) everywhere.

Owens tends to be only partially understood. Her early plays, *Futz, The Karl Marx Play,* and many others were performed in Off-Broadway avant-garde theatre to much critical acclaim. Most audience members and readers understand and embrace the outrage, the absurdity, and the overt in-your-face energies – but they have a hard time explaining their emotional reactions. For audiences who prefer the type of poem or play that imposes order onto chaos, and comforts one with a highly predictable set of characters, behaviors, and outcomes, to read or observe a performance of Owens's work can be unsettling.

And yet, in a world where science advances through multiple working hypotheses, and where each seemingly obvious causal chain is a target of questioning, Owens's work stands as a representative of the unseen processes at work. The lack of a firm and final ending point can be challenging, though. Nevertheless, at a time when individuals' narratives of explanation are at best highly metaphorical coping strategies, it is more important than ever to understand and embrace works of literature that reflect the highly charged, rapidly shape-shifting underlying processes.

Susan Smith Nash, Ph.D.

I. New Poems

DEVOUR NOT THE ELEPHANT

Poaching scene
crime scene carcasses of
dead rhinos and Savannah elephants

Precious the ivory tusks and horns
cut off severed

Two from a bull
raw and bleeding holes gouged
into Jumbo's face

Swollen infected the wounds
every day bears the data

Data of body
feces hair and nails yellowish-white
bones push to the surface

In the green of leaves Earth
Air Fire Water

*

What is property?
property is the body Ears Trunk
Feet

The face half-severed precious
the ivory tusks and horns

Property is the body
mutilated burned Ears Trunk
Feet

Ears like human fingerprints

none are the same

Flapping their ears
blood circulates in the head
ears the shape of Africa

Two long pointed teeth stick out
of the mouth

The trunk is like a human arm
or the fingers of a hand
picking berries

Elephant corpses found drifting
In a creek yellowish-white bones

Push to the surface
In the green of leaves Earth
Air Fire Water

What is property? property
is the body a human arm or hand

My mother was sold
from me when I could
but crawl

*

Among the stalls
piles of ivory trinkets bangles
and beads

Rows of Ivory carvings
of maidens monks and birds

Carcasses of dead rhinos
and Savannah Elephants carcasses

stripped of their skin

Burned mutilated saleable parts
hacked off

Ears Trunk Feet
the horns and tusks ground up
my body the bread my blood the wine

*

Disturbingly informative
an elephant savaged by poachers

Poison in the rivers
poison in the arrow heads following
the dying animal around

Following the dying animal around
every day bears the data

Data of body body of data
property is the body mutilated burned
carnal/spiritual

In the green of leaves Earth
Air Fire Water

[N.B. To which she adds, in correspondence: "The elephant is a non-predatory mammal, a sensate being. The poem intersects body and spirit -- elephant desire, with the function of marketing, production, distribution and exchange of elephant and rhino body parts by human predators."]

BELOVED THE AARDVARK

The letters horizontal
or vertical f l o a t before
your eyes

a black line shapes itself
spells out the first noun in
an english dictionary

with a forefinger and thumb
spells out A a r d v a r k
an animal from Africa

body of data data of body
rabbitlike ears a long cylindrical
tongue

the tail of a kangaroo
nocturnal burrowing a member
of the mammalian order

made of the parts
of different animals lay your hand
feel the bones under the skin

*

The universe contains
everything that exists letters
that spell out

r u i n s c a p e

end to end long strings
of words blinking in and out
as the universe contracts

e x p a n d s

across the twenty-first century
mounds of sand appear
disappear

always the Aardvark moves
in circles moves in circles
in the here and now

swaying side to side
massive the claws digging
searching

work is a binding obligation
a jaw opens and closes
carnal/spiritual

*

On a computer screen
reflections of water metal glass
bouncing radio waves

black lines form letters
precise methodical long strings
of words vertical/horizontal

words detached from
the course of events planned
or spontaneous patterns

spirals of wind and fire
zigzags of black and white lines
layers of brown dust

biomorphic geomorphic

polymorphic slashes slashes
of solar light

earth air fire water

motionless the Aardvark
stands listening blood in
blood out

*

Press button to see
Science and Art of creating
archetypal scenes

come into being
long ago an hour ago
only a minute

known and unknown shapes
the flesh of the apple the dome
of a human skull

a mushroom cloud

each successive image
signs and wonders earth air
fire water

motionless the Aardvark
stands listening blood in
blood out

*

Press button to see
a bucolic setting grape vines

olive groves

fields of sunflowers
white the summer blossoms
a wedding party

the bride and groom pale
and red his lips her breast vein
as thick as a finger

out of his mouth
protrudes his tongue cinnamon cumin
honey and salt

lines of insects appear
disappear tendons and nerves
pulsate

a flow of hormonal forces
blood in blood out the universe
contracting

e x p a n d i n g

an outline shapes itself
playful the unborn babe in its
amniotic sac

*

Always the Aardvark
moves in circles moves in circles
in the here and now

earth air fire water

moves in circles swaying
side to side rhythmic the blood

the months in a year

disease famine torture war

mounds of sand appear disappear

massive the claws
digging searching long ago
an hour ago

only a minute

*

On a warm day in spring
a woman plays a harpsichord
the lid painted with scenes

of mythological animals
known and unknown shapes
nocturnal solitary

black zigzags
appear disappear motionless
the Aardvark stands

listening a jaw opens
and closes audible inaudible
the sound of the predator

lay your hand
feel the bones under the skin
carnal/spiritual

*

Next to a wall
of concrete stands a man

covered with tattoos

orange yellow green
astrological signs etched into
his skin

tendons and nerves
drink color his hand balled
into a fist

a fringe of drool
and blood circles the mouth
his lips move

a secret tribal language

then he counts
the months in a year his thumb
and forefinger moving

back and forth along a wall

'who eat up my people as they
eat bread'

*

Morning to evening
evening to morning audible
inaudible

the rhythm the rhythm
of spontaneous changes sunlight/
blackness

blinking in and out

piles of sand appear

disappear audible inaudible
the sound of digging

digging deeper
precise methodical searching
always the Aardvark

moves in circles moves in circles
in the here and now

swaying side to side

piles of sand appear
disappear work is a binding
obligation

suffer the Aardvark children

*

Out of an ant hill
a waft of air lovely the ant hill
curved like an embrace

*

Rays of sunlight
penetrate the roof of your skull
warming your back

warming your hands
and fingers holding a piece
of charcoal

drawing zigzags of
black lines tendons nerves
ligament

spirals of veins pulsate
blood in blood out

*

On a concrete wall
lit up by fluorescent light
vibrating particles

shape the contours of an animal

the face of the Aardvark
is its parts the eyes nose
and mouth

the cylindrical tongue

the long ears
heating to the temperature
of human skin

*

Pale and red
the mouth of a child eating
an apple

a montage of bite marks

your hand balled into a fist

*

Press button to hear
morning to evening evening
to morning

a s o u n d s c a p e

of everlasting duration
evening to morning morning
to evening

out of the digital age

a course of events
the scientific explosive realm
across

the twenty-first century

*

Press button
to hear a musical interval
in the afternoon

sipping Umbrian wine

tearing off the wing
of a roast pigeon a musical
montage

evoking the rhythm
the rhythm of spontaneous changes
Louis Armstrong's

"Black and Blue"
a Bach cantata Native American flutes
Buddhist chants singing dolphins

Willie Nelson's "On the Road Again"

*

You turn in

the direction of a voice
spelling out a word

A m f a t t e h r

a voice repeating
an unknown word motionless
the Aardvark

stands listening
a voice repeating spelling
out a word

A m f a t t e h r

made of the letters
of a noun drawing zigzags
of black lines

horizontal/vertical

a piece of charcoal
held with fingers and thumb
body of data

data of body
an animal from Africa
a member

of the mammalian order

*

Mounds of sand
appear disappear massive
the claws digging

searching

long ago an hour ago
only a minute

the universe contracts e x p a n d s

disease famine torture war

rhythmic a flow
of hormonal forces blood in
blood out

disease famine torture war

the Aardvark
comes out in daylight to lie
in the sun

*

Evolution is smart
clean clear and simple gaps
in the sequence of

events laid down and eroded away

hungry or thirsty
eat or drink body of data
data of body

audible inaudible
the rhythm the rhythm of
spontaneous change

letters spell out

o b l i t e r a t e

a jaw opens and closes

carnal/spiritual

vigilant the babe sucking

*

On a giant computer
screen vibrating subatomic
particles shape

the contours of a skull

and in your
mammalian brain tendons
and nerves pulsate

craving licking
burning chunks rupturing flesh
cinnamon cumin and honey

five lambs
slaughtered for the feast
carnal/spiritual

*

Under an occult sky
of greens and yellows the tattoo
artist bites into an apple

chewing and swallowing
moisture and nutrients flow in
the tattoo artist's brain

seized with jittery energy

chewing and swallowing
inhaling exhaling a layer of skin

the skin

a montage of bite marks

chewing and swallowing
inhaling exhaling the breath blowing
kisses along the digestive tract

spirals of veins
pulsate from mouth to rectum
blood in blood out

seized with jittery energy

chewing and swallowing
inhaling exhaling drawing zigzags
of black lines

a layer of skin the skin
the canvas absorbing sunlight
inhaling exhaling

drawing zigzags
of black lines drawing a fetal skull
sprouting tooth buds

the universe
contains everything that exists
letters that spell out

r u i n s c a p e

*

After waking
and lying down trust your
instinctual senses

disturbingly informative

tears mucus
albumen a goat smile
on your lips

*

Long ago
an hour ago only a minute
in the here and now

in the zone diverging from
a course of events

spirals of wind and fire

layers of brown dust

*

Out of an ant hill
curved like an embrace
a waft of air

and morning
to evening and evening
to morning

audible inaudible
an unknown word letters
that spell out

A m f a t t e h r

*

The bones that form
the Aardvark Venus rays of light

penetrate your fingers

drawing black lines
spirals of muscles blood vessels
a long cylindrical tongue

biomorphic geomorphic
polymorphic corkscrews of white
smoke

slashes slashes of solar light

*

Long ago an hour ago
only a minute a black line
shapes itself

an image on a rock
subatomic particles pulsate
the universe contracts

e x p a n d s

*

The warmest of mothers
moves in circles massive her claws
digging searching

body of data data
of body the Aardvark Venus
her rabbitlike ears

heating to the
temperature of human skin
a long cylindrical tongue

work is a binding obligation

blood in blood out
her breast vein as thick as a finger
mounds of sand appear

disappear
lines of ants appear disappear
a hissing sound

suffer the Aardvark children

*

Listening to Willie Nelson
you witness a lovely desert sunset
a goat smile on your lips

mounds of sand appear
disappear and morning to evening
evening to morning

9 breakfasts 5 lunches 6 dinners

white the summer blossoms
a girl in your arms hungry or thirsty
eat and drink

*

On the wall of a cave
in the Sahara in a zone diverging
from a course of events

disease famine torture war

in a sacred refuge or a tomb

Behold! the Aardvark Venus

luminous the overlapping
charcoal drawings charcoal fed
with wind and fire

charcoal fed with blood and sunlight

*

Earth Air Fire Water

hormonal forces evoke
the rhythm of spontaneous change
inhaling exhaling

moisture and nutrients
flow through your mammalian brain
inhaling exhaling

the universe contracts e x p a n d s

seized with jittery energy

inhaling exhaling
flexing contracting evoking
the rhythm

the rhythm of spontaneous change

disease famine torture war

rays of light
penetrate your vulva scrotum
sphincter

illuminate your heart

your hand cupping
the little god mounds of sand
appear disappear

out of an ant hill
curved like an embrace
            Earth Air Fire Water

SOLARPOETICS

Earth Air Fire Water

1

Wyh do we udnersntad a txet eevn fi the letetrs
aer in dsiordre

*

The letter A
like a membrane
melliferous the animal flesh
bread baking   butchery

Alphabet of blood and ash

Litany   incantation
from the back part of her throat
salt for the stew   salt
for the bread

Sings the *poète maudite*

When I in my youth
strolled in a blue wool dress
I strolled in a circle of blue

2

The reading brain the eyes moving constantly
while reading

*

The letter B
when black letters of fire
patterns of animus across
the landscape

The place in the distance

Where the air
smells of poisoned rain
take one step after
the other

Where you do not want to go

An amalgam of words
in sequential order here where
you walk ahead   stop
raise your eyes

3

We identify only ten or twelve letters   quick jumps
three or four letters left and seven or eight letters right

*

The letter C circles
zigzags   animates the plaster
death cast   a solitary
workwoman then

From the back part of her throat

When I in my youth in a blue wool dress
I strolled among maidens   monks
and birds   I strolled in wind
cold and heat

Across green volcanic hills

There In shadows   haze   smoke
in three dimensional space   piles of charred
human and animal bones

4

The history of the neurology of reading
the existence of a visual center

*

The letter D whispered
in the dismal quarter where
absence of a picture   the green
volcanic hills

Grain   grape   bread   wine

The story of the shepherdess
staged and scripted sub-plots there
in a bucolic setting our lady grows
out of a mound of dirt

Her rose-bud mouth a crooked line

A breast vein as thick as a finger
the wedding feast   bread and meat
yellow   sulfurous   a plume
of smoke

5

Some written words lit up or hidden among
geometric forms

*

The letter E
elaborate the graphic design
chasms and fissures
in the earth

Our lady grows out of rotting meat

Sings the *poète maudite*
I in my youth   concealed and disguised
walked in three dimensional
space

Heat   cold   wind   water

Data science
pain   fear   phobia   multimedia
exhibitions   photographic art   illustrations
the ritual of baking bread

6

Yeast spores are ubiquitous in air and on
the surface of grain

*

The letter F
the preserved body rotates forms
sweet bacteria then the skin
of the fingertips

Chemical   molecular where

In a circle they joined hands
ruiners and destroyers engulf and consume
victims and executioners ooze out
the urge

Staged and scripted sub-plots

Genesis to revelation
in elaborate letters shift twist and slant
disease famine torture war
earth air fire water

7

Everything begins in the retina
ten years of research on the reading brain

*

The letter G a graphic design
sight   touch   listen   the sound
of grinding corn   the smell
of bread baking

Then she brews tea over a fire

There in reddish violet light
violet light   a jagged black line zigzags
a graphic design   the head covered
with a hood

Identity unknown   tree   rope   grain

The air smells of smoked meat
his mouth waters   taste buds pulsate
from a gap   a fissure a flow
of hormonal forces

8

Begin to understand
the nature of the leavening process

*

The letter H
catches in the throat   then she steps
backwards and flings
a handful of earth beyond the edges

Of a page   you hear a hollow sound

The dry external covering
of an ear of corn   then stepping forwards
she scatters letters cut out from
the skull   spine bones

The form of a human body

When I in my youth
in a blue wool dress   I strolled
in a circle of blue
sings the poète maudite

9

The cerebral cortex   a sliver of brain
barely thicker than a credit card

*

The letter I vertical
 under an occult sky once upon
 a time I sat cross-legged
 In the crotch of a tree

Grape   wine grain bread

From roots of plants
that bear the grain in darkness
light heat cold   focus on
a common scene

Chasms in the fissured earth

The story of the baker
a set of skills in sequential order
the finished loaf A to Z
in place and space

10

Recognize in some dozens of milliseconds
a written word

*

The letter J the shape
of a hook and on the hook
the butcher's coat
wind heat cold drought

Blood and mud flows out of the right sleeve

One animal
gut head and tail   measure
body length jaws claws
diameters of holes

The zones of inclusion exclusion

Salt for the stew salt for the bread
once upon a time my mother
was sold from me when I
could but crawl

11

Dispatches from the frontiers of neuroscience

*

The letter K stands apart
like a barley plant
in three dimensional space
the dry external covering

A snarl of fibrous hairs

Drifting in circles
wind heat cold drought
and dead white the barley plant
cut down

Deboned and buried

Then the reading brain
follows one letter after another
beyond the edges
of a page

12

One millionth of a second an episode
and of the volume of bread eighty percent is empty
space

*

The letter L a right angle
walk down a street
step by step blood pushes
to the surface

On your tongue a metallic taste

Flour and water
yellow sulfurous a plume
of smoke I strolled in wind cold
and heat

Drifting geometries

Between victim and executioner
t h e r u i n s c a p e
the eyes move constantly while
reading body of data

13

Networks of neurons organize themselves
chemical molecular

*

The letter M vibrates in
the earth hums the rhythm
of spontaneous
change

Slapping flying insects Insects

Far and near spiritual hole
animal soul a secret tribal language
work is a binding obligation focus
on a common scene

A plume of smoke

Bread baking butchery
microbes in a petri dish a method
of colonizing and
dispersing

14

The ability to bridge gaps utilizing data science
and drawing connections

*

The letter N remembers
once upon a time
on the sea bed strange
scars

A black line zigzags

Zones of inclusion exclusion
the reading brain eyes
moving constantly
pinpoint

A selected shape

A circle a hole a fat fold
of the abdomen a breast vein
as thick as a finger
a loaf of bread

15

All the letters are in nature the forms that
our cortex chooses

*

The letter O is a hole
that engulfs consumes gut
head and tail one
animal

The pit of mayhem

Out of the digital age
a set of skills in sequential order
body of data data
of body

Rhythmic the flow of hormonal forces

Edible the heart tongue
and liver sings the *poète maudite*
salt for the stew salt
for the bread

16

Reading a word does not depend on the number
of letters it contains

*

The letter P periodic orbital
biological compulsion
like taste and thirst
and in your

Mammalian brain

Lovely the pastoral scene
a graphic design
green the volcanic hills
the story

Of the shepherdess

In elaborate lettering
heat cold wind water
a flow of menstrual
blood

17

The stereotype of a lone researcher
in a secluded lab--a science fiction trope

*

The letter Q a quartet
in three dimensional space
the butcher baker shepherdess
a solitary workwoman

Ravenous her lidless eye

Counting letters spelling
m e l l i f e r o u s the animal flesh
the flow of hormonal
forces

Blood in blood out

From A to Z a set of skills
body of data data
of body gut head tail
o b l i t e r a t e d

18

An experiment designed to control the brain
--movements of limbs with colored lights

*

The letter R under a red
violet light an unknown figure
crouches over the
earth

Where the air smells of poisoned rain

An unknown figure digs rows
of small holes the temperature
of human skin folds
in the ground

The root of love

Blood in blood out
folds in the ground from front
to back from back to
front

19

Electrical pokes regulate balance direction
currents moving neuron to neuron

*

The letter S serpentine
the organ of sight a pair of spherical
bodies in an orbit of the skull
the eyes

Nomads wanderers

Take one step after
the other here where you walk
bones push to the
surface

A snarl of fibrous hairs drifting

In circles chasms and fissures
in the earth   holes gaps in a sequence
of events laid down and eroded
away

20

Begin with a few humble ingredients rice flour
fruit and flowers

*

The letter T near a tank
with a spigot stands the baker
collecting words batter
crumbs

Black mold burnt rolls

Dead white the bakers lips
on his tongue a metallic
taste more water
in the loaf

Less flour used

The story of the baker
A set of skills in sequential order
from A to Z   O wicked
world

21

All words may be reproduced stored in a retrieval
system
or transmitted in any form or by any means

*

The letter U numberless
tree stumps mark a sequence
of events rows of
holes

Absence of a picture

A story of the solitary
workwoman long ago an hour ago
only a minute strolling in
autumnal leaves

Drifting in circles

And in your mammalian brain
lovely the pastoral scene
grain grape bread
wine

22

Colors forms movement all together an astonishing
neurological image

*

The letter V gouged
into a stone floor blood pushing
to the surface zones of
inclusion exclusion

Here where archeologists

Observe dimensions between
victim and executioner a gap a fissure
a hole that engulfs and
consumes

Here where historians

Pouring coffee organize
body of data data of body piles
of charred human and animal
bones

23

Evolution is smart clean clear and simple
hungry or thirsty eat or drink

*

The letter W when your
eyes move the reading brain
the act of reading how tightly
the letters hold you

Wind heat cold drought

Hot exuberant the butcher's
pleasure cutting deboning grinding
salt for the stew salt
for the bread

Sings the *poète maudite*

From point A to Z a set of skills
in sequential order blood
and mud chemical
molecular

24

With sophisticated equipment scientists scrutinize
minutiae gathering information

*

The letter X
marks an unknown figure
behind an electric
fence

Patterns of animus

A skeletal frame
crouches over the earth
fingers spreading apart across
t h e r u i n s c a p e

Hidden among geometric forms
a single bloodstained feather
long ago an hour ago
only a minute

25

The two cortex regions operate independently
of each other independent yet intertwined
.
*

The letter Y yellow
sulfurous a plume of smoke
work is a binding
obligation

Looking to earn extra cash

Take one step after
the other under an occult sky
the hand of the butcher
lops off

Diseased parts

Slapping flying insects insects
far and near hair and nails in the feces
vulnerable flesh-eater spiritual
carnivore

Ever-pinging networks twenty-six letters of the
alphabet
asterik to zero hour

*

The letter Z a sound
of a buzz saw strange scars
on the sea bed patterns
of animus

Written words lit up

Hidden zigzags
burned buried premonitions
take one step after
the other

Out of the hole of Baudelaire

When I in my youth
strolled in a blue wool dress
I strolled in a circle
of blue

DE CHIRICO'S VENDETTA

In this story detached
from the course of events
staged and scripted

out of a lost narrative

figures in these scenes appear
            d i s a p p e a r

*

My room is a divine pilgrimage
s c u o l a   m e t a f i s i c a

*

De Chirico stands
in front of a blackened wall
morning to evening

evening to morning
painting a town bisected
by a railroad

drawing a tailor's dummy

painting vertical/horizontal
lines shadows of a blackened wall
brighter darker

squares rectangles circles
a ferocious s c a t t e r i n g
blood in blood out

spirals of colors pulsate
moisture and nutrients flow
in your mammalian brain

you listen to recordings
of his voice watch his gestures
facial expressions

an Italian from Genoa or Egypt

whistling humming---
lontano lontano his body sways
side to side

the universe contracts
            e x p a n d s

blinking in and out
vibrating subatomic particles
fill the dome of your skull

disease famine torture war

the universe contracts
            e x p a n d s

a glass of ice water sparkles

his tongue protrudes
from your mouth and you taste
the rain

De Chirico shifts his gaze

*

When drawing ovals

his father's face appears
                d i s a p p e a r s

audible inaudible
repetitions of words---you must find
the demon in everything

black and hot my coffee

white and cold my women
painting trains empty walkways
a toga clad manikin

seized with jittery energy

he makes a fist phallus
work is a binding obligation
painting morning

to evening evening
to morning painting a deserted
townscape painting

an armless female statue

desire suspended
between observer and subject

humming---lontano lontano

audible inaudible
moving your lips as you read---
contempt scorn ridicule

writing in his journal
I Giorgio De Chirico amputated
at the knees---

the Art dealers
s t r a n g l e   h o l d

painting a black silhouette
a train emerges from a brick wall
he makes a fig sign

De Chirico shifts his gaze

*

In Las Vegas displayed
in a shop window a series
of self portraits

from a marble bust
back dated f o r g e r i e s
of early works titled

with the name De Chirico

also multiple paintings
from his Metaphysical Period
back dated f o r g e r i e s

titled with the name De Chirico

also a hundred drawings
of Towers Of Loss back dated
f o r g e r i e s

titled with the name De Chirico

fake De Chirico paintings
made by De Chirico work is
a binding obligation

*

When at Piazza Santa Croce
rays of light penetrated the palms
of your hands when

blood congealed

pushed to the surface
S t i g m a t a
R e v e l a t i o n

De Chirico shifts his gaze

*

Internal disorders
are neither logical nor illogical
neither are biscuits

in the middle of a rectangle

moisture and nutrients
flow in your mammalian brain
drawing crayfish

oysters eggs eyeballs

clusters of bananas
a bull's testicles a scrotal vein
as thick as a finger

and there came
a violent spasm in his gut---
painting baguettes

lying in a coffin box

the dome of a skull

M i t o   T r a g e d i a

and he paints
ornamental letters spelling
i m m o r a l   f o o d

seized with jittery energy

you must find the demon
in everything laughing drinking
vino he draws

a black iron skillet

glowing particles
of charred fish skin humming---
lontano lontano

De Chirico shifts his gaze

*

At the edge of
a deserted townscape
his father's house

longing thrown onto
the canvas morning to evening
evening to morning

an outline shapes itself
            e n i g m a t i c
scenes come into being

black and hot my
coffee white and cold
my women

how to view still life

the spasms of death
to view how life still his body
sways side to side

you must find the demon
in everything you must find the demon
In broken geometric forms

De Chirico shifts his gaze

Author's note.
Giorgio De Chirico, a pioneer of Surrealism was greatly admired for his early works, his later paintings from 1945 to 1962 drew the disdain of fickle dealers who influenced collectors. Thus, De Chirico decided to back date the paintings.

George Economou and Rochelle Owens, Greece, 2006

EVERLASTING DURATION,
IN MEMORY OF GEORGE

You are sitting down
to a late lunch
in my castle on a hill

while a jazz trio plays

then suddenly
a chemical reaction
takes place---

and you smell
the scent of roses and feel
my hair growing

on every part of your skin

but not the palms
of my hands or the soles
of your feet

Day One

I am standing
in front of a group of musicians
controlling

the speed of sound

then suddenly
a chemical reaction
takes place---

saliva pools behind
your teeth   sinuous the rhythms
under my skin

your lips move

audible   inaudible
and I begin to chant a secret
tribal language

Day Two

In a triangle of haze
and smoke I am following
a marching band

appear and disappear

then suddenly
a chemical reaction
takes place---

spirals of veins pulsate
nerves and tendons drink color
sight   smell   taste

pale and red your lips

my tongue protrudes
from your mouth and I taste
the rain

Day Three

You are hanging
upside down and side to side
I swing

earth   air   fire   water

then suddenly
a chemical reaction
takes place---

I am a barley plant
cut down   dead white the barley
plant cut down

you are a pouched mammal

attached to a nipple
mother and father crawled
onto the land

Day Four

I am flapping
my right hand and your left
hand is balled into a fist

the universe contracts   e x p a n d s

then suddenly
a chemical reaction
takes place---

the smell of saffron
and lilac   morning to evening
evening to morning

milk of the mother misery

milk of the father terror
vigilant the babe   sucking   carnal/
spiritual

Day Five

Through the gaps
of my fingers vibrating subatomic
particles blink in and out

vertical/ horizontal

then suddenly
a chemical reaction
takes place---

a breast vein
as thick as a finger   amorous
the greedy seed

every day bears the data

grain   grape   bread
and wine   your skeletal frame
the limbs spreading apart

Day Six

Behind you
a black line appears   disappears
a latent image

a wall of brown dust

then suddenly
a chemical reaction
takes place---

a black line curved
like an embrace   lay your hand
feel the bones

under my skin

your sculpted pelvis
vertical/ horizontal   corkscrews
of white smoke

Day Seven

In the twenty-first century
the here-and-now   in the zone
diverging

from a course of events

then suddenly
a chemical reaction takes
place---

a metallic taste on
my tongue   I am an old
woman

sipping black tea

you are a little boy
sitting cross-legged under
a dead blue glow

OUR RUINSCAPE

On the cover
of a Science magazine
a rare image

disturbingly informative

you stare down
pursing your lips your neck
to the side

plagued by doubt

a hologram
of the skeleton of a horse--
I must not jump-the-gun

*

The rapt reader stands
in the space of an enigma
the hidden contours

of raw data

*

Under a dead blue glow
a laboratory technician observes
a configuration of microbes

rapidly zigzagging

zigzagging microbes
in a petri dish colonizing dispersing
precise methodical

biological compulsion

*

“O Maggie you wrecked my bed
then kicked me in the head”

The love of logic
the logic of love I must not
jump the gun

*

ZIgzags of black lines
circles triangles rectangles
subatomic particles
                                        f l o a t i n g
on a computer screen

molecular the art
of nature amorphous the forms--
corkscrews of white smoke

blinking in and out

the spiral tail of a comet
charred bits of the rat’s thigh
a dog gnawing a bone

*

Earth yields dandelion
yields lemon trees moisture
and nutrients

a flow of hormonal forces

amorous the greedy seed
craving licking nectar milk mucus
rhythmic the ecstasy

carnal/spiritual

leaves and limbs
          s p r e a d i n g
                    u n d u l a t i n g

on multiple screens
digital images the body
of the tapeworm

folding folding into itself

undulating
          s e g m e n t i n g
blowing kisses along
the digestive tract folding
folding into itself
               u n d u l a t i n g
                    s e g m e n t i n g

Earth Air Fire Water

*

An outline shapes itself
playful the unborn babe in its
amniotic sac

carnal/spiritual

*

Morning to evening
evening to morning under

the mask

a smell of decay

eye scape ear scape
                    r u i n s c a p e

*

Your bulbous tongue
hangs like a drape over your lip
the pulsating fissures

rapidly zigzagging

zigzagging fire ants etch
maps of wrath and anguish
                    a c r o s s
your martyred
blood-packed tongue

*

End to end a c r o s s
the triumphant twenty-first
century

out of the digital age

through the gaps of
your fingers the mute eyewitness
sees hanging in the sky

the skeleton of a horse

appear disappear
eye scape ear scape
                    r u i n s c a p e

*

"O Maggie you wrecked my bed
then kicked me in the head"

the love of logic
the logic of love I must not
jump the gun

*

A laboratory technician
draws a circular mark passing
her hands measuring

counting dividing

numbering the bones
skull neck spinal column
yellow the bones

laid out like stage props

one for the cat chasing
a rat one for the dog gnawing
a bone

*

The universe contains
everything that exists---biomorphic
geomorphic polymorphic

Earth Air Fire Water

the universe contracts
                                        e x p a n d s

every day bears the data
disease famine torture war

*

It is at dusk when
through the gaps of your fingers
you see peculiar forms

when an outline shapes itself
appears
                    d i s a p p e a r s

the stump of a tree splits

vertical/horizontal

it is at dusk when
through the gaps of your fingers
an old woman on horseback

appears d i s a p p e a r s

when through the gaps
of your fingers the mute eye witness
sees hanging in the sky

the skeleton of a horse

appear d i s a p p e a r

*

Evoking the rhythm of
rhythm of spontaneous changes
dead cells

clothe and feed the flies

totem and taboo totem
and taboo work is a binding
obligation

blood in blood out

*

Rays of solar light pass
through the dome of your skull
rows of cadavers

when every dawn
each day dead cells clothe
and feed the flies

flashes of solar light
illuminate prehistoric forests
rows of cadavers

when every dawn
each day dead cells clothe
and feed the flies

rays of solar light
pass through layers of water
rows of cadavers

when every dawn
each day dead cells clothe
and feed the flies

rays of solar light
pass through a barley plant
rows of cadavers

when every dawn
each day dead cells clothe

and feed the flies

beams of solar light
penetrate volcanos glaciers deserts
rows of cadavers

when every dawn
each day dead cells clothe
and feed the flies

rays of solar light
spiral into a mushroom cloud
rows of cadavers

when every dawn
each day dead cells clothe
and feed the flies

beams of solar light
break down concrete walls
rows of cadavers

when every dawn
each day dead cells clothe
and feed the flies

rays of solar light
burn through plastic particles
rows of cadavers

when every dawn
each day dead cells clothe
and feed the flies

flashes of solar light
split the sea of plastic particles
rows of cadavers

when every dawn
each day dead cells clothe
and feed the flies

beams of solar light
snake dance into plastic particles
rows of cadavers

when every dawn
each day dead cells clothe
and feed the flies

beams of solar light
break up dwarf storms of plastic particles
rows of cadavers

when every dawn
each day dead cells clothe
and feed the flies

flashes of solar light
spiral through plastic particles
rows of cadavers

when every dawn
each day dead cells clothe
and feed the flies

rays of solar light
pass through volcanic hills
illuminate a single

blood-stained feather

when every dawn
each day dead cells clothe
and feed the flies

*

Out of the scientific
explosive realm the triumphant
twenty-first century

out of the digital age

every day bears the data
black letters spell
r u i n s c a p e

II. Three Poems in French

HORISHI

Souhaitant l' e u p h o r i e

tourmenté par l'envie de Van Gogh

le tatoueur commence à tailler

un tournesol

une couche de p e a u

la peau la t o i l e

absorbant le soleil

les pétales s' é c a r t e n t

chaque piqûre le globe oculaire

les pouces les doigts de Van Gogh

marquant la p e a u

injectant des colorants

la peau la t o i l e

absorbant le soleil

chaque pétale teint en jaune

une touche de vert et de blanc

d'un seul coup

une auréole bleue brillante

le feuillage d'or du coeur

du soleil

la signature mystique

la signature mystique de Van Gogh

cachée entre les cuisses du guerrier samourai

le mot l'énergie du L o g o s

l'encre le sang

la peau transpercée par les épines

la peau la t o i l e

absorbant le soleil

le bruit des aiguilles

l'ondulation des vagues

des vagues et du vent

la peau la t o i l e

absorbant le soleil

****

LA FEMME DE JESUS

C'est la peau et des cheveux

de la maîtresse yoga de Rosario au Portugal

Souviens-toi lorsque j'ai dit que ses cheveux

étaient une longue corde sinueuse

tombant sur sa clavicule

sous l'épaule

une longue corde

sinueuse

tombant

sur sa poitrine

Désireuse la peau la peau déchirée

comme les pétales de fleurs

Désireux les couteaux du Portugal

répétitifs rythmiques monotones

les os coupés la chair pourrie

Souviens-toi lorsque j'ai dit que la peau

rugueuse les cellules mortes des cheveux

répandues transformées

devenues bourgeon

un bourgeon devenu fleur

un lys vert pâle sortant de la boue

où se reproduisent des huîtres

la boue de Rosario au Portugal

Souviens-toi lorsque j'ai dit la lumière

rosée d'une pâleur spectrale

sa peau sa chevelure

Souviens-toi lorsque j'ai dit sa voix ensorcelante

sa voix rapide sa voix disant

"les Portugais sont de grand voyageurs"

Souviens–toi lorsque j'ai dit qu'elle avait baigné

les corps des amputés

enveloppant

leurs members de bandages

qu'elle avait soigné et fait vivre

nourrissant les mutilés

aux mutilés des accidents

aux mutilés des accidents de chemin de fer

de voiture

aux mutilés de guerre

Souviens-toi lorsque j'ai dit qu'elle fredonnait

et chantait en portugais

en attachant leur prothèse

elle fredonnait et chantait

les voyant reprendre vie

se levant de la tombe comme Lazare

comme Lazare sortant de la tombe

Ses bontés bannissant le mal de monde

la lumière rosée d'une pâleur spectrale

Souviens-toi lorsque j'ai dit qu'elle avait rêvé

d'un taureau noir du Portugal

les jambes amputées

elle avait rêvé d'une naine riant

le visage pur

la lumière rosée d'une pâleur spectrale

Il s'agit de Barbara de Jesus

de Rosario Portugal

elle se trouvait devant une ruche

une ruche d'abeilles

elle écoutait le travail du coeur

la lumière rosée d'une pâleur spectrale

la maîtresse yoga respirait

les étudiants respiraient en étendant leurs mains

comme les danseuses balinaises

des cellules mortes de cheveux

répandues transformées

Souviens-toi lorsque j'ai dit qu'elle s'etait assise

sur son talon

chantant chantant chantant

lingam yoni vida morte

lingam yoni vida morte

lingam yoni vida morte

la lumière rosée d'une pâleur spectrale

****

LE CERVEAU PRIMAIRE

Voilà une sculpture

en bois taillé

c'est Marie-Madeleine

Marie-Madeleine

dans la lumière violette

Devant la sainte

la belle pénitente

se trouve un monstre

de couleurs vivantes

de signes astrologiques

c'est un monstre qui s'appelle

Gila –Gila

lui aussi dans la lumière violette

pour rendre homage

pour rendre homage à la sainte

Voilà un beau reptile de couleurs vivantes

de signes astrologiques

d'une forme majesteuse

dont le cerveau compose

un vrai poème élégiaque

Voilà Marie-Madeleine

Marie-Madeleine la belle pénitente

tous les deux

sans péché

dans la lumière violette

III. Not Be Essence that Cannot Be

A collection

Reprinted from the 1961 edition
New York City: Trobar

BELONGED INTO SHEEPSHANK

Hunger
It is luck too. Hullabaloo Vishnu
Knowledge birds liturgic liverwort dynamite ne-not
Hideous Munt Jak
Barbarous.
Rosy.
Like emblem on the teeth. Two, the best
I pray thee, the nose leaking, the indians, the words
And songs
Nimble feeted.
Enlightened
Be a cold
Thing.
The same time. Tied to no place
Belonged into Sheepshank punjabi delusion
Unreal with no
Thing.
Lived.
Which my Pope. Bent over
Made pregnant ordained bursted the good
Fat foreskin
After entombment
And carpfishes.
Tonkin
Mere not Simon Magus. He was emptied
Before the man and animal mentally again and again
Between the hole of the mouth
And ass hole.
The base salty.
Some matter. I emit
I hold value and attached butter-fat love
Good selfishness
Burnt clay.
Unclearly christian
For a hump.

UP UP ON THE DISORDERS OF THE HAIRS

The least be be oaklike colorless. Or. Or the
Sweat ducts hither hither Come. Up the nostrils
Tangled incredible. On this genus brass. Yellow.
Being touched hither hither hither hither flat-
Footedness, focus on this genus brass. Yellow.
Yellowish in the fe-male. In the huckleberry.
By the dry withdraw-al.

Get out out the booms, fingers and toes, in the
Arctic friiz of vigor middle finger. That on
The Yucca horse and ass, zinc and male or like
Jove, joyey cheek through the air METHINKS be-
Comes suckling pigs down down on the prickli-
Ness. Up Up on the disorders of the hairs.
Give an eating oil.

CALLED ALSO THE INSTANT

Become limulus sounded minuted Gradual the silent lumps
Worst silent Become limulus Which one which one Which
Other divi-ded Magni-ficent Made spiry
The Maker The kind Judas six of Jul-ius
Receiving O mimicry Zarin pith deigned deigned without
Worst The foretelling Joseph Smith four feet
In answerable Called also The instant Also the trembling
Umbel Tyrr Manx cat And forefoot
Of And profanation Two Kings shown two spheres reached
Placed And After Her Of it Tallow Tasmania con-verted
Who Who in the fetter That
Is far less Other things The count-ry shrubs and trees

(BOM) ONLY CHECKERBERRY

(Pukist)
    Behold!
            (Winter)
            (Winter)
Ned.
Dog. Nigra. Boodle
Dulia. Pungent. Pelidna dum
Dum. Work
Mediterranean
Mediterranean
Gloominess
(Pagouros)
Crasy Shakespeares
Midsummer
Jynx
Past and wrong
(Bom) only checkerberry
Yields shits (cucumis)
                (Winter)
                    (Winter)
Spicy red berries (winter)
                    (winter)
Wart hog joy.

NOT BE ESSENCE THAT CANNOT BE

ME Agonizes. It it's Brown ME
Which treads, changes, Agonizes. This
   Desmodium Venturous. Than the other
            (From a tick). Infinite Not Be.
Not Be essence That cannot be escaped. ME
It's brown carnivorous Burrowing Is the like
Beyond Beyond. Illimitable. Outrageous. Known.
Mediocre Mediocre.

SAY OLD ENGLISH WISHE ME

th th
twease my paws My voice her tits
was loafs of bread just dadabeeyah
sap south-pole jipa savejoy
three bladders say old english
wishe me
sweet-loss
suck lent drool
infallible
meat broke
scab lip lips whistling
with the nose
beget rejib   horrible in th
th th
pencil wish me twitch
sea raven
just
dadabeeyah

MA NIP (GO AWAY)

my bullet ma be a good gel
   MA KISS FLAGRANTLY
Ma nip (go away) slightly
nebuLOUSEly miMICKing
like a shadow (butcher)
coMINGing on Shekinah
carving the Slovaks man nananimal
man nananimal
   Slaz the harvest fly's
hard meat HARD 'nd harmless
ma I'm natural (but)
Ma nip (go away) slightly

LOST TENDING TO ICCHEN YICCHEN

He
Heads
Tiger Eye,
Hawse hole,
Name enclosed in
Cob nut,
Sir Henry in Habana
Cuba. Suckblood.
The stems and stalks,
Them human heat lighters
Heart land. Health Eaters.

Make
Of Georgians
Holy piss of the
Caucasus
Formula . . Is Atomic
Suborders
In urine and india rubber,
Affected in anger, Family gu-blow
The same other number 2 shit
In indigo and kindness
We unnerve not offensive.

Culture,
Milk,
Soil, serum,
Vatican Councils,
Three bones
In organik
Enos, penos, muscle
By intimation
Free mercy wholly
Inmeshed, Loco and chiefly

Lawful.

Any genus
Misty mastered.
Go send Mishnayoth
His wrong minus semi
Parasitic American
Pipefish,
Sharp point charges,
Money shevism pinchcock,
Trees spurious flow fluids.
Common likened (Hypopitys)
Not significant and genuine.

Fertilization
Wife,
Fenugreek,
Sugarman with water inch
Identical (poison ivy). Jack
It's fictitious
Ithun Ithun. Lost tending to
Icchen Yicchen body of
Eboris Myrna that object
Of ginseng saturation,
The fruit mulberry yellow-wood.

An
Jaloos
No-Ah. Like radical
Kangaroo Hence time
On the balls Jackass
Neck feathers
Reversed forming
Bright blue and
Naught ropes, wire
2 minerals
Jad Jad Devotees.

Origin
Of Zebedee.
Myth. Pal. Serving the
Shape mixture of Japonia,
(Native knuckle over the front
Double fist)
Obsequious young latex
Scriptures,
Udders,
Midst
Soldiers, Arms, (Mimosa).

That ore
Nor vegetable old,
Mine mals sights, mass
Phases only old world
And the seeds remote.
5 devine offspring ale-wife,
(Peace Esox Grinus) Holy place
Spoilt.
Peely head developed
Chirp buttercups poagrass
Daringly bountiful.

ZU ZU MIDDAY I'M NARCOTIC

Endlong skirmish lump
I am gallant, greek
Nightingale, zu zu
Midday I'm narcotic,
Light, ball-flowered
Fly, ku ku ven-emous
Beyond wood luring
Stick, polled, over

My mucous, meaning
Many me's hot-short
Poor snakemouth I
Sence eels sneering
My forward voo doo
To and fro, seven
puffs, to and fro
ME, white-colored

YOU muck luck dope
A evil drink, top
Of a wapiti poyo,
YOU goo me bloodshot
YOU whacky fop, O Oph
Elia you milk the
Pocket-knife poko
On holidays in the sun

I'LL STILL HAVE

be jeered at
spot brown
on me
& harass
i'm putrid
i'm lowest
(i suffer meanly)
of them with the symbol
alway
& my nose is inflamed
roasted meat
lap the drippings
(i should not)
have the   brown
on me
O openly
nocuous
not ever kiss
& give up
buzzing away
(speaking distinctly)
to the bare ear
(O my long tai1)
i'll still
have   i'I1 have
Nizam
& jaw & nose
my gut wall
one foot Iong

DRIPPING THING FOUR LEGS

Till she's dead, cult-
Ivated (zool zool) lady's
Finger upon her, waiting
Forming sweet bacteria
Dripping Thing Four
Legs between Needed
Four legs Great Maria

Insanity. And the alco-
Holic Not satiable high
Ner-vous hindiihideous
Cr-ime, exaggerated.
Woman. In ripening no
Accomplishment Head with-
Out Urine Harsh absol-

Ute. Yupun cedar Crotch.
Of a human being Actively
Cool. Risen piggishly Conk-
Ed Supported jeered, involv-
Ing knotgrass branches as
Come out two serpents kill-
Ing. With pipes. Pink and

Stinking Forth. Below. Mam-
Mals Either lick of a group
Side of bad female propagated
With a war-m day of spring Afri-
Cans unfeeling-ly think of fo-
Od Meat dried hard. Eat-en
By men and women Hook the shank.

AB BRANCHES OF TREES

Udo Udo sto-
Ut, wilted
Vital snot
(In the urine, eyelashes)
(In the sack, big rnonoto-
Nous snot, again)

Unsegmented, we croak
Wax cylinder to remember
Us by Hebdomadal fuck you
Lame as a game dog
(In a woman's shape)
(Contains eternal tick fever
Thuja. Bear it)

Croak you ag-
Ain seasons, ab bran-
Ches of trees, noose
Fastened, unkempt
Swinging (In a organism, gray white
Goose-fit)

HERA HERA HERA

You Ye; The bee's jail, Puck workhouse
YOU YE zealous spongy devoting to
Fucking logic, bath-ing in the
Stream, giggling. Laying pros
Titutes lowly, Mary Eddy
Lengthwise, Mahatma the beholder,
Relieving trickiness above one leap year
Eating cucumber. Opposed to the crotch crotch
Hucking honeybee
Boiling the ruuts
The hognut lower down mewing
Screwing, The giant ragweed,
And feeling the loneliness
Staining
Yellow green.
Crookneck with bark whorish
Europe bones divide
Mad shame and kissing
Sweetmeats. My lord very good
In the mind
You Ye whose
Crack open
After after after sap drain, stealth, Hera Hera
Hera

O WAFERSH TASHTE GOOD

o 6) o glutinous
o glot of glory
do an earthquake
o shockhead (50ft)
piss backward b
o special friend
twice o chrissakes,
b o natural man
(again in confession o wafersh tashte good)
shlike new, sho pleashe!
fixsh my marriagesh
everyshling allright
shknock shknock help!
shling shling
a brigadier shcould
it, itsh sho bad
o engineershz fixsh
(fluk hurricane was bad weather shtoilet shlike)
it itsh shzown shthe
MY FLUSH, stush
hung mush (Mrs) agony
cooed o bridesmad
crosh a fem and o
monthly maN is bad
o thief o shush
(Mrs) agony hung
(an animal pick worthy pick jist in jail breath)
out skullcap breed
o agony cooed
(Mrs)

BRUISE YOU NOT HONEYCOMB

By you I ting
the thing make tree kang
aroo, for, three
muscle
in
wheatworm, mary-josher, papIo reversionary. Be eating
and sore big
son-sin
sin-son
g
day of a babylonia
bag in coptifity, bacteria caught everybody
to contrary me
Gas, bruise you bruise you
not honeycomb or mama not-Czech
Oslop oslop 0 shove
with a pang in
Kings and the queens baby wagging their three vomits
and spice wet
fin-gers
tut-oo-war
f
novaskoshia and eleven bones
not a shrub sick and all likeable and naked
contemplative with skrotums
Billy-america sit on ground plum
peeling a pleasant shit socking the fresh water
Oos Osoos soo
or suffering
for the mango language matter of innocence around the trunk
of the tree
phaglagala
merry-and-big
h

ROCHELLE OWENS

A central figure in the international avant-garde for fifty years, Rochelle Owens is a poet, playwright, translator, and video artist. She has published eighteen books of poetry including *Hermaphropoetics, Drifting Geometries* (Singing Horse Press, 2017), *Out of Ur: New & Selected Poems 1961-2012* (Shearsman Books, 2013), *Solitary Workwoman* (Junction Press, 2011), and *Luca: Discourse on Life and Death* (Junction Press, 2001). She is the author of four collections of plays and also edited *Spontaneous Combustion: Eight New American Plays.* She translated Liliane Atlan's *The Passersby.* Owens has been a recipient of five Village Voice Obie awards and Honors from the New York Drama Critics Circle. A pioneer in the American experimental theatre, her plays have been presented at Le Festival d'Avignon and the Berlin Theatre Festival. She is widely known as one of the most innovative and controversial writers of this century, whose groundbreaking work has influenced subsequent experimental poets and playwrights.

www.ingramcontent.com/pod-product-compliance
Lightning Source LLC
LaVergne TN
LVHW041259080426
835510LV00009B/806